The Old Church Book

The Old Church Book

Robin Langley Sommer

BARNES
& NOBLE
BOOKS
NEW YORK

Page 1 photograph:
A rooftop guardian angel adorns Old Montreal's Chapel of Notre-Dame-des-Bon-Secours.

Page 2 photograph:
An elegant community church in scenic Watts River, Vermont.

These pages:
The steeple of Boston's Old North Church (Christ Church), 1723

This edition published by Barnes & Noble, Inc., by arrangement with Saraband Inc.

1999 Barnes & Noble Books

Design © Ziga Design

Library of Congress Cataloging in Publication Data available

ISBN: 0-7607-1406-1

Printed in China

10 9 8 7 6 5 4 3 2 1

IN MEMORIAM

PASTOR DOUGLAS F. VERDIN
AND
THE REVEREND CANON
LEONARD A. CRAGG

Contents

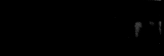

Introduction

Unto thee, O Lord, do I lift up my soul.

— PSALM 25

The historic churches of North America, in all their diversity of materials, styles and religious traditions, are among the most beautiful and cherished features of our built environment. Each one has a story to tell, whether of immigration from Europe to attain freedom of worship, settlements made in the hope of evangelizing the native nations, or ethnic spiritual ties transplanted to a new homeland to serve as the focal point of community life. Many of these buildings are still in use today, having changed in style, but not in spirit, over the course of generations.

New England church architecture, which has deep affinities with that of Atlantic Canada, offers a microcosm of the changes wrought by time, population growth, new influences on architecture and the proliferation of sects and denominations in the New World. The original meetinghouses of the Puritan Congregational faith were built in Massachusetts in the seventeenth and early eighteenth centuries after the establishment of Plymouth, Salem and Boston. The Puritans founded a theocracy that did not distinguish between sacred and civil law. Their gathering places served for town meetings as well as communal worship and forswore the embellishments of the Anglican faith they had left behind, including the longitudinal basilica plan focused upon an altar. The first meetinghouses were generally square wooden structures with hip roofs rising to a central cupola and spare interiors in which the pulpit predominated.

Between about 1710 and 1800, the oblong, barnlike meetinghouse with a gabled roof and frontal tower became the norm. The focus remained on the pulpit, opposite the entrance, and the steeple and belfry were in the classical style of the late-blooming English Renaissance.

After 1800 the churches we usually identify as "New England style" were built widely

Opposite: *A simple wooden belfry adorns Holy Trinity Church in Trinidad, California (1873).*

Below: *Our Lady of Good Voyage, Gloucester, Massachusetts (1914).*

throughout the northern colonies. A porch or portico was added to the façade, with columns, pilasters, or other ornamentation, and the multi-staged steeple incorporated round-arched openings, low balusters and tall, narrow spires. As the Greek Revival style gained popularity after the American Revolutionary War, the familiar wooden church was sometimes executed in stone, with Doric columns, a wide frieze and a sturdier bell tower crowned by a cupola. This type was most prevalent around urban areas like Boston, where both architectural fashion and the growth of Anglican, Baptist and Unitarian congregations diversified regional architecture.

After the U.S. Constitution was established in 1789, its First Amendment forbade the adoption of an officially established church. Freedom of worship was guaranteed not only for democratic, but for pragmatic reasons: religious wars had torn Europe apart for centuries, from the Reformation, begun in Germany by Martin Luther (1517), through the Counter Reformation of the powerful Roman Catholic monarchies. Pluralism became the hallmark of the American religious experience, while Canada adhered more closely to its two original traditions: Roman Catholicism in what was known as New France until the British conquest of Quebec in 1759, and Anglicanism (called Episcopalianism in the United States) with the arrival of English-speaking settlers and emigrant New Englanders from the mid-eighteenth century onward.

Right: *An early, simple adobe Mission chapel in the desert near Santa Fe, New Mexico. The city's Spanish name means Holy Faith.*

Left: *A missionary chapel, whose construction resembles a Native American lodge of the Great Lakes region, preserved at Green Bay, Wisconsin, recalls the era of French exploration and evangelization among the Huron.*

The first great classical styles in both the United States and Canada originated in the Italian Renaissance with the architect Andrea Palladio (1518–80). He studied the remains of Roman architecture and made carefully measured drawings that served as the basis for his work *I Quattro libri dell' architectura* (Venice, 1570). It outlined practical systems of classical design and proportioning that were widely circulated in both Europe and England.

Most of Palladio's buildings were executed in and around Vicenza, where he built grand townhouses in brick and stucco rather than marble, with pilasters, columns and two-story porticoes in the classical mode, raised on a rusticated platform. In Venice, he built such churches as San Giorgio Maggiore and the Church of the Redentore. In the seventeenth century, the great English architect Inigo Jones imported the Palladian style to his country, where it would influence the work of church architects including Christopher Wren and, later, James Gibbs of the Georgian period (1714–1820). Exported to the New World, Palladian classicism manifested itself in the Georgian, Federal and Neoclassical styles, and its influence is still seen in Colonial Revival architecture.

Among the English Renaissance churches that had a major impact on North American ecclesiastical architecture were Christopher Wren's landmark St. Paul's Cathedral, in London, begun in 1675, and James Gibbs's St.-Martin-in-the-Field and St.-Mary-le-Strand, also located in the British capital. Design elements from these structures dominated English-speaking regions from Atlantic Canada down to the Deep South, where they overlapped with the Spanish colonial architecture of St. Augustine and Pensacola, Florida, whose influence once reached as far north as the Carolinas. In the Southwest, Spanish colonial Baroque styles and vernacular adobe-construction techniques merged with those of the indigenous peoples to produce the Spanish Mission church, found in several forms from New Mexico to northern California.

The early nineteenth century saw the ascendance of the Greek Revival style, based on new knowledge of Greek and Roman architecture gleaned from archaeological work on original sites, rather than adaptations of Renaissance models. Churches resembling tiny Greek temples were erected in both stone and wood, the latter frequently painted white to simulate the look

Opposite: *The spirit of New England in Peacham, Vermont.*

Below: *The historic Friends Meetinghouse in Philadelphia, built by Quakers who were welcomed to William Penn's liberal colony of Pennsylvania.*

of Grecian marble. As westward migration increased, the style was carried across the continent, reaching its peak before the Civil War. At the same time, new ethnic groups brought elements of their original styles to the construction of churches in both urban and rural areas. The growth of sectarianism contributed to the diversity of church architecture, as pointed out by historian Marilyn J. Chiat in *America's Religious Architecture* (John Wiley & Sons, 1997):

"Ethnic groups as different as Mormon and Yankee have their origins in America. But even with the proliferation of religious sects, the intertwining of religious and ethnic identities...remained visible. At one time a small market town in Minnesota had five Lutheran churches: Swedish, Norwegian, German, Finnish and English. The latter was established by the children of immigrants who had intermarried and chose not to affiliate with an ethnic congregation. Completing the town's religious and ethnic composition were two Roman Catholic churches, one German and the other Irish, and a Methodist congregation established by a circuit-riding minister. It was the heartland's version of Wilder's *Our Town.*"

As prosperity and population increased throughout the nineteenth century, a host of Victorian-era styles succeeded one another and, almost as frequently, combined with one another in the eclectic spirit of the time. Some of them, including the French Second Empire style of the 1870s, were little suited to church architecture, while others, especially the Gothic Revival style, increased in influence throughout the century. From its introduction during the 1830s through its apogee as the ornate High Victorian Gothic of urban cathedrals and fashionable resorts, the perpendicular medieval style popularized by John Ruskin in England became the dominant influence. American architects A.J. Davis, Ithiel Town and Richard Upjohn were instrumental in establishing the Gothic Revival style as the reigning mode for church architecture.

As in residential architecture, Gothic churches might comprise other elements, from the Romanesque Revival to the picturesque Queen Anne style, but the basic form has remained popular to the present day with congregations who seek "something that looks like a church," rather than an austere Modern or innovative Postmodern building.

The plates that follow feature a representative cross-section of North American houses of worship, from log-cabin missions in remote Western outposts to the historic French Renaissance cathedrals of Montreal and St. Louis, Missouri. The rich and diversified splendor of our architectural heritage is nowhere more apparent than it is in the beautiful old churches that comprise an eloquent living testimony to our spiritual and communal history.

Traditional New England Styles

The purity and simplicity of the New England colonial church is a distinctive feature of North American architecture. This unmistakable style, with many variations of detail and decoration, had its roots in the Protestant Reformation, and specifically in the Anglican Church, which displaced the Church of Rome in England during the reign of Henry VIII (1491–1547). By the early 1600s, many dissenters had become dissatisfied with the liturgy and hierarchy of the established Church of England, comparing it to the Roman Catholic Church in its emphasis on temporal rather than spiritual power.

Most of these dissenters were from both the laboring and middle classes rather than the aristocracy, and they were persecuted for their resistance to the state religion. The Puritans sought to divest the church of pomp and other vestiges of "Popery" by simplifying its creed and ceremonies. The Quakers, Baptists and Separatists believed that the established church should be replaced by freedom to worship according to one's own spiritual guidance, within the context of the Judeo-Christian scriptures. It was these motivations that brought many devout Englishmen to the New World, including the Pilgrims and Separatists, who arrived in Plymouth, Massachusetts, in 1620. Eight years later the Puritans disembarked to settle at Salem, and in 1630, Puritan colonists founded the city of Boston. Over the next ten years, some 20,000 more people came from England to settle present-day Lynn, Roxbury, Watertown and Dorchester, Massachusetts.

Human nature, in its perverse way, soon manifested itself in the form of exclusivity on the part of the Puritans, who became even more intolerant of other religious views than the Anglican Church had been of theirs. Even the Quakers, who were committed to nonviolence and equality in "the good light" they ascribed to the Holy Spirit, were harangued and beaten; some were killed. When members of the Massachusetts colony, including Roger Williams and Anne Hutchinson, objected to this intolerance, they were driven out. During the 1630s, they established the first settlements in what is now Rhode Island, where religious freedom was a reality. At about the same time, a group of Puritans led by Thomas Hooker left Massachusetts to settle in the fertile Connecticut River valley. New Hampshire, too, was colonized by dissatisfied members of the original Massachusetts Puritan community. In all of the early colonies except Rhode Island, which was settled mainly by Baptists, the Congregational Church was the official religion, and its emphasis on simplicity, piety and good order was reflected in its houses of worship and in the autonomy of each community, which made its decisions without reference to bishops or presbyters.

The original New England churches were nearly always square, unpainted wooden buildings, framed in oak that was mortised and tenoned with axes so that it could be pegged together. Most had four-sided hip roofs that rose to a central belfry, perhaps surrounded by a balustrade. The exterior walls were weatherproofed with clapboarding, and the interiors

Opposite: *Harmonious colonial-style churches framed by October's richly colored foliage in Grafton, Massachusetts.*

Above: *America's oldest surviving Puritan meetinghouse— the Old Ship Church, in Hingham, Massachusetts, begun in 1681.*

were usually roughly plastered. Sometimes a ceiling was installed at the level of the eaves, and seating consisted of backless benches on either side, which were occupied by men and women, respectively. Later, backs were added to the benches, some of which evolved into square enclosures, or box pews, adjacent to the walls. The central space and gallery were filled with open pews that faced the pulpit.

No one is sure who designed these early buildings, but by the mid-seventeenth century they had risen in Boston and the adjacent Bay communities. The fact that they served for public gatherings as well as services is reflected in the name "meetinghouse." Unfortunately, only one of these original meetinghouses has survived: the famous "Old Ship Church," built in 1681 in Hingham, Massachusetts. Its diamond-paned windows recall the time when glass was a scarce commodity in the colonies; its preservation recalls the origins of a new experiment in theocracy on this continent.

From about 1710, beginning in Connecticut, Massachusetts and New Hampshire, a radical departure in church architecture manifested itself before the religious revival described as the Great Awakening, initiated by Jonathan

Edwards in 1732. Meetinghouses of the new type were rectangular, with a spired tower at one end, and were built in the classical style that dominated both English and French architecture during the 1700s. Most had the main entrance on one side and moderately sloped gable roofs. The influence of the great English architect Inigo Jones (1573–1652) was felt across the Atlantic, and the plain, clear lines of Georgian architecture struck a responsive chord in New England Congregationalists. Working primarily in wood, they placed round-arched Palladian windows and doors along the façade and the sides of the building. Classical columns or pilasters rarely appeared until the early nineteenth century; ornamentation was minimal and restrained. The steeple was usually at the front, either part of a square tower projecting from the façade, or set at the peak of the roof. It was staged in squares and polygons of classical inspiration, often articulated by arched openings and balustrades, and the white spire sometimes rose to a height that made it visible for miles. This, in fact, is the prototype of what we usually consider the New England style.

Many fine examples survive, as seen in the following plates, although the interiors have been altered and realtered over time. Perhaps the finest extant meetinghouse of this kind is Boston's Old South Church, built in brick in 1729. It replaced an earlier church on the same site—called the "Old Brick"—and surpassed it in size, growing from 72 by 54 feet to 95 by 68 feet. This increase in floor space—almost 70 percent—to serve larger congregations was achieved by abandoning the four-sided roof in favor of a pitched roof, which entailed placing the belfry in a tower added at one end. In some cases, the tower became a separate structure. The need for a larger worship space goes far to explain the replacement of the hip-roofed, essentially medieval-style, meetinghouse with a church more closely attuned to the classical style of the mother country.

American builders relied on several books by English and colonial architects, including the *Book of Architecture* by the London ecclesiastical architect James Gibbs, and the *Country Builder's Assistant*, written by Asher Benjamin, a carpenter-architect born in Greenfield, Massachusetts. Thus the majority of the eighteenth-century New England churches were designed by local craftsmen whose names, for the most part, are unknown to us. Notable churches designed before the American Revolutionary War and still standing include the Congregational Church in East Haven, Connecticut (1772); the "Old North Vestry" (c. 1711) in Nantucket, Massachusetts; and the Hampstead, New Hampshire, Old Meetinghouse (1745), which now serves as the Town Hall.

Other denominations grew slowly in New England, but they, too, built their houses of worship and adhered to the tenets of their faith communities. Strangely enough, the Church of England made slow headway, even in cities like Boston and New Haven, despite its sanction by the Crown and the membership of many wealthy merchants, officials, sea captains and military men. Boston Puritans were mortally offended when Governor Edmund Andros intruded upon the Old South Meetinghouse in 1687 to hold Episcopal services. The shock in New Haven, Connecticut, was greater still when most faculty members of Yale College, founded by the

Congregationalists, announced their conversion to Episcopacy in 1722 and left for England to take holy orders. As Yale president Theodore Woolsey wrote long afterward: "I suppose that greater alarm would scarcely be awakened now if the theological faculty of Yale were to declare for the Church of Rome, avow their belief in transubstantiation and pray to the Virgin Mary."

Above: *Boston's Old South Meetinghouse, built in 1729 to replace the original brick church on this site.*

Left: *Wickford, Rhode Island's, Old Narragansett Meetinghouse, built in 1707, features Palladian ground-floor windows and a classical entryway.*

The Church of England soon gained more adherents in Connecticut, where some forty-two parishes had been founded before 1776. It grew more slowly in Massachusetts, where Boston's King's Chapel was the first Episcopal church built in the colonies (1689), but the wealth of its membership and tokens of royal favor from overseas soon resulted in several excellent church buildings. In 1749 King's Chapel was replaced by the present building, designed by Newport architect Peter Harrison and built of Quincy granite, with a plain tower in front. Forty years later, an imposing classical colonnade was built around the base of the tower. A chancel projects from the back of the church, which has two tiers of windows. Even after the congregation became the nation's first to accept Unitarianism, the serene interior was left virtually unchanged, except that the focal point moved from the altar to the ele-

gant "wineglass" pulpit, backed by Corinthian columns rising in pairs to the vaulted ceiling.

Boston's oldest surviving church is the Episcopal Christ Church, built in 1723 and reportedly designed by a city print dealer named William Price. This handsome brick structure has a projecting tower at the front, housing a peal of eight bells imported from England. Two square stages above the belfry are topped by a spire, which was blown off in the hurricane of 1804 and rebuilt under the auspices of Charles Bulfinch, whose architectural stamp is clearly visible in this historic city. The influence of the original design is reflected in Newport's Trinity Church, which is also congruent with the Congregational churches of the period.

In Rhode Island, the Baptists were free to practice their faith, and many of their churches have survived, although most were altered to reflect later styles, including the Greek Revival, Gothic and eclectic Victorian. Providence has several noteworthy Baptist churches, including the First Baptist (1775), the third meetinghouse of the church founded by Roger Williams, whose members originally worshipped in one another's homes, like the Amish of Pennsylvania. This time-honored building is a square structure, unusual in having doors on all four sides. The tower projects from the west end of the peaked roof, and its base is enclosed by a deep porch. Two rows of round-headed windows encircle the building. Newport has a variety of Christian churches, including St. Paul's Methodist (1806) and the Seventh Day Baptist (1729, now incorporated into another building), as well as the nation's first synagogue, called Touro Synagogue (1763) for the congregation's founding rabbi, Isaac Touro. Today it houses Temple Jeshuat Israel.

The Society of Friends, commonly called the Quakers, played a vital part in the religious life of colonial New England, and at least twenty of their simple meetinghouses have survived. Typically, they have two doors, one for men, the other for women, and a gallery encircling the interior. As architectural historian Edmund W. Sinnott observes in *Meetinghouse & Church in Early New England* (McGraw-Hill, 1963), "The

Below: *The atypical Round Church (actually polygonal) built in Richmond, Vermont, between 1812 and 1814.*

Friends made no great contributions to meetinghouse architecture. The houses they erected, however, have a simplicity and charm that to many is as attractive as the columned portico or ornamented steeple of the Puritan church." Examples of the Friends meetinghouse can be found in Portsmouth, Rhode Island (1700); North Pembroke, Massachusetts (1706); Dover, New Hampshire (1768); and South Uxbridge, Massachusetts (1776).

When the Revolutionary War broke out, many Quakers emigrated to Atlantic Canada because of their pacifist convictions, along with the Loyalists who rejected the Revolution on political grounds. A colony of Quaker whalers from Nantucket was welcomed to Nova Scotia, where they built their customary saltbox-style homes and frame meetinghouses, which were entirely in keeping with the vernacular wooden architecture of the region. One of these settlers was William Ray, who enlarged a house on Octerlong Street in Dartmouth that is now part of the Dartmouth Heritage Museum.

Newcomers from New England were augmented by many settlers from the British Isles, skilled in both woodworking and masonry traditions, who contributed to the beauty of the built landscape in Upper Canada, Nova Scotia and the newly created colony of New Brunswick. While Protestants had been excluded from Catholic New France since its foundation, the capture of Quebec by the British in 1759 brought growing numbers of British settlers imbued with the ideals of classical design to shape both French and British building styles in Canada.

Post-Revolutionary church architecture in the former colonies retained its earlier form with some modifications. Rather than a tower projecting from the façade, New Englanders began to add a porch or portico, with columns or pilasters at the main end and a single or double entrance. The tower was generally set into the front peak of the gabled roof. Often, a Greek pediment with a dentiled cornice line occurred in both the portico and the gable end of the roofline. Ornamentation, seen in the form of Palladian windows, fanlights, louvered open-

ings in the steeple, and gilded domes, became more elaborate on early nineteenth-century churches. The most influential architects of the day were Asher Benjamin, mentioned earlier, who began his career as a country carpenter and built many fine churches in New Hampshire, Vermont and Massachusetts; the eminent Charles Bulfinch; Ithiel Town, who worked with Benjamin on the plan for New Haven's Center Church; and Salem's Samuel McIntire, who built both beautiful houses and the town's South Church (1803, demolished). The indigenous Federal style took precedence over Georgian classicism, associated with Great Britain, after the Revolutionary War, and by 1830, the influence of the popular Greek Revival and the styles that succeeded it, as discussed in subsequent chapters, became increasingly apparent in New England church architecture.

Below: *The First Congregational Church of Chatham, Massachusetts.*

Historic Colonial Meetinghouses

The 1787 meetinghouse at Rockingham, Vermont (right), and the venerable 1772 Harrington Meetinghouse in Pemaquid, Maine (opposite, below), are simple frame clapboard buildings that served for both religious and communal gatherings. Immediately adjacent to the buildings is the cemetery, as seen at Pemaquid and, below, at the New England-style Red Church in Tivoli, New York (1752).

A Style for All Seasons

The commonalities of clean, simple design in wooden construction unite these churches from several different periods. Above, the First Congregational Church of Stonington, Connecticut, founded in 1674; opposite, a nineteenth-century Anglican church at Lac Baker, New Brunswick, with fishing shacks in the foreground; left, the Lakeville (Connecticut) United Methodist Church (1816), with Gothic Revival detailing and a cornice line inspired by Greek prototypes.

Classical Steeples

Beautiful multistage steeples inspired by late-Renaissance English prototypes crown these historic churches. Above is the Wilton (Connecticut) Congregational Church, dating from 1790; on the opposite page is the clapboard Old Baptist Meetinghouse (1796) in North Yarmouth, Maine.

Regional Landmarks *overleaf*

The New Preston (Connecticut) Congregational Church with eclectic Victorian decoration dates from the mid-nineteenth century (left), and the Congregational Church (right) at Stowe, Vermont, has Greek Revival features including the gable pediment and pilasters.

Images on the Water

The busy harbor at Camden, Maine (opposite), is overlooked by the town's serene white nineteenth-century church, with a clock face below the tall spire. The Congregational Church in Newfane, Vermont, below, has a graceful three-stage steeple reflected in the quiet pond behind the building.

Connecticut's Puritan Heritage

Opposite, below, is Enfield's Old Meetinghouse (founded 1775, altered 1800s), with its statue of local Revolutionary War hero Captain Thomas Abbey. Above, and opposite, above, are two nineteenth-century churches, the first in East Canaan and the second in Saugatuck.

In Wood and Stone

The Peru, Massachusetts, Congregational Church (1846), below, has a square belfry crowned by Gothic-style crenelation and finials. Ridgefield, Connecticut's, beautiful fieldstone Episcopal Church, St. Stephen's (opposite), was partly burned by British troops during the Battle of Ridgefield (April 27, 1777). The restored church features a Greek Revival portico and Palladian tower windows.

Frontal Towers with Balustrades

These examples from two New England states share the Palladian-style steeple crowning a square frontal tower. Opposite, Trinity Episcopal Church (1726), Newport, Rhode Island; and below, Strafford, Vermont, Town Hall (1799), which was formerly a meetinghouse.

Enduring Presences *overleaf*

The Congregational Church in Old Bennington, Vermont (left), built in 1805, was designed by architect Lavius Fillmore. The Warren (Connecticut) Congregational Church (right), has an unusual fish-shaped weathervane and a handsome entrance bay comprising four pilasters and triple doors (1818).

Humble and Proud

The vernacular First Baptist Church (left) in Chester, Vermont, with pointed Gothic windows and a modest square belfry, takes its place beside two Massachusetts landmarks. On the opposite page is the Stockbridge Congregational Church, founded by Jonathan Edwards and built by Ralph Bigelow in 1824. In the same year, architect Winthrop Clapp designed the Unitarian Church below (called the Brick Church) in historic Old Deerfield.

Folk Churches and Meetinghouses

Modest folk churches and meetinghouses across the continent, most of them built by their congregations, testify to the faith of the immigrants from many lands who peopled North America. Their denominations were diverse, but their dedication was single-minded. Most adhered to the creeds in which they had been raised, and their ethnicity was expressed in their sacred places.

Roman Catholics from New France to Hispanic California built vernacular churches rooted in the Latin rite, often of cruciform shape and always oriented toward the altar, where the sacramental mystery of the Eucharist, or thanksgiving, was enacted. Most of these churches were named for a patron saint, or for a major Christian belief like the Holy Trinity or the seven sacraments. They housed artefacts traditional to the faith, whether in simple or elaborate forms: crucifixes, statues, votive and altar candles, and bas-relief plaques or pictures depicting the fourteen Stations of the Cross that memorialize Christ's Passion and death. Every church had a baptismal font for the rite of infant baptism and a pulpit from which the Gospel was proclaimed by an ordained priest. In remote and mission areas, which had no resident priest, mass was said when a missionary priest visited the area, much as some Methodist communities relied on a "circuit rider" to officiate at their services.

Orthodox Catholics from eastern Europe, the Middle East and the Balkans built churches in the Byzantine or Eastern-rite style, with onion-shaped domes, repetitive arches and Greek-cross motifs (equal-armed crosses at right angles to the center). Their focus, too, was on the altar, which had an openwork screen (iconostasis) hung with lamps and sacred images between the celebrant at the altar and the congregation. Except for monastics, the Orthodox clergy did not practice celibacy, and their families took an active part in the community's spiritual life. Their original vernacular churches were built in major cities like Chicago and in remote ouposts of Alaska and the Canadian prairie provinces, settled respectively by Russian Orthodox and Ukrainian immigrants. Greek Orthodox immigrants are memorialized by the shrine to St. Photios, originally built in 1743, at St. Augustine, Florida.

Opposite: *Tiny St. John's United Church on Miscou Island, New Brunswick, also serves as the island's lighthouse.*

Left: *This humble log structure is a reconstruction of the Czech Catholic Holy Rosary Church built on the site, in Texas, in 1856.*

Pioneers from Germany and Scandinavia established many Lutheran churches in the Midwest and on the Plains, from Ohio and Indiana through Iowa, Missouri, Kansas, Nebraska and the Dakotas. Their styles, too, were influenced not only by their European building traditions, but also by the New World's climate, topography, available materials and the prosperity or poverty of a given congregation. As in most of the major Protestant sects, the pulpit was the focal point for scripture reading and preaching, while the congregation took part in spoken and sung prayers and in such sacraments as baptism, confirmation, marriage and holy communion.

In the South, originally settled by English colonists, with a significant Spanish presence in Florida, the Baptist religion eventually became dominant and remains so to this day. From West Virginia down through Alabama, Mississippi and parts of Louisiana, many simple, unadorned Baptist churches reflect the austere tenets of this faith, with its emphasis on accountability, morality and the doctrine of original sin redeemed by grace. Major civil rights leaders, including Marthin Luther King, Jr., have emerged from the Baptist community to stir the conscience of the nation.

Among the many Baptist sects and congregations are those founded by African Americans

after the Civil War. In West Virginia's Kanawha Valley, the African Zion Baptist Church, a frame structure on a stone foundation, with a modest louvered bell tower, was the state's first spiritual home for African-American Baptists. Booker T. Washington was one of its members, and its founder was "Father" Lewis Rice, a leader of the local black commmunity, who had ministered to its members when they were still enslaved. The sanctuary has changed little since its dedication in 1872.

The African Methodist Episcopal Church also gained many adherents, both before and after the Civil War. A church for black Christians was founded on Baltimore's Orchard Street in 1839 by a former slave named Trueman Le Pratt, and the African Methodist Episcopal Church was established eight years later by free blacks in Cumberland, Maryland. Their first church was a modest frame structure built in 1848, which was replaced in 1892 by a larger brick building that is still in use. The denomination spread widely as blacks migrated to the Northern states in search of better living conditions. There is a flourishing A.M.E. congregation in the writer's hometown in southwestern Connecticut.

In Utah and the Mountain states, the Mormon religion became increasingly prevalent after the foundation of Salt Lake City, the new Zion, during the 1840s. The Church of Jesus Christ of Latter-day Saints, as it is more properly called, was zealous in its missionary work both at home and abroad, and its Temple and Tabernacle in Salt Lake City are world famous. However, the majority of Mormon churches, or ward meetinghouses, were built in rural areas from native materials like brick, logs, frame and slab (squared logs). One example that has been preserved is in the town of Chesterfield, Idaho, which has been unoccupied for some years. The rectangular brick meetinghouse has a hipped porch and a gabled roof with a half-round lunette window in the front gable containing the dedication date 1892. The structure is maintained as a museum by the local Daughters of Utah Pioneers.

Below: *An isolated chapel on South Carolina's St. Helena Island showing the influence of Spanish Florida.*

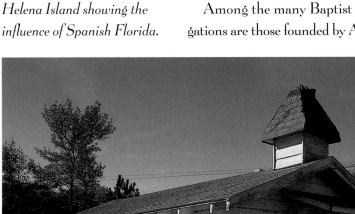

The Methodist Church was also active in missionary work, and many converts were made at outdoor revival meetings conducted by circuit riders sent out by the Methodist Society of America, founded in Baltimore in 1784. The Methodist Tabernacle near Mathews, Virginia, erected in 1922, is one of the state's few remaining revival shelters: a two-story, hip-roofed frame structure supported on posts, and open to the outdoors on all four sides. As the church became established, it moved west with the pioneers, building its houses of worship in the styles and materials of the regions settled.

Settlers from Scotland brought their Presbyterian faith to the New World during colonial times, and were influential from New England to the Natchez Trace by 1790. Nashville, Tennessee, on the Cumberland River, established in 1779, became the new point of departure on the Natchez tribe's historic 600-mile pathway from the Cumberland to the Mississippi rivers. Tennessee's oldest Presbyterian congregation was founded in Washington County by a Scots-Irish minister named Samuel Doak in 1780. Its original modest church bears little resemblance to the exotic Old First Presbyterian Church built in Nashville by architect William Strickland in the new Egyptian Revival style in 1851. The Presbyterians were especially active in missionary work among Native Americans, as seen in the Wheelock Mission Presbyterian Church in McCurtain County, Oklahoma (1846). Its founder, the Reverend Alfred Wright, worked with the Choctaw in Mississippi until their forcible deportation to what was then known as Indian Territory on the infamous "trail of tears." Their first worship space was outdoors, on benches made of split logs facing a wooden-box pulpit. Log buildings were soon constructed, and in 1846 the present stone church—Oklahoma's oldest—was completed. The rectangular building has a simple stepped entryway flanked by narrow windows and a wooden steeple thirty-five feet tall. There is a vaulted ceiling over the main floor and balcony, and the pews and pulpit were hand carved by the congregants, who also chiseled the local stone for the exterior walls, which are almost two feet thick.

The New World attracted many sects who formed close-knit, self-sufficient communities centered around their spiritual life. Among the best known are the Shakers, who diverged from the English Quakers in 1797. They established a number of communities in New England shortly thereafter. Named for their zealous liturgical dancing, they became respected as successful farmers and craftspeople, who did everything, as St. Paul had enjoined, "with [their] whole hearts." They practiced celibacy, so their

Below: *The Friends Meetinghouse in Olympia, Washington, is a fine example of the simple Quaker style, transported west from New England and the mid-Atlantic states.*

Right: *A small shrine in the wooden vernacular style of Atlantic Canada, with clapboard cladding and Gothic detailing.*

Right: *A small shrine in the wooden vernacular style of Atlantic Canada, with clapboard cladding and Gothic detailing.*

Opposite: *The Art United Methodist Church (1890) overlooks a field of bluebonnets in Art, Texas.*

Below: *The Russian Orthodox Church in Bethel, Alaska, with a domelike roof ornament and separate bell tower.*

growth was limited to converts, and their numbers dwindled during the later nineteenth century. The last active communities were at Canterbury, New Hampshire, and Sabbathday Lake (New Gloucester), Maine. The Shaker Meetinghouse at Canterbury (1792) is characteristic of their simple style: a two-story, gambrel-roofed building of white clapboard, with twin chimneys and dormers on the lower roof slope. There are separate entrances for men and women. The worship space is on the ground floor and other community rooms occupy the upper level. It is reported that while they erected the building, the workmen maintained a reverent silence, speaking only as necessary to further the task. The inevitable disappearance of the Shaker faith community is a sad loss to America's spiritual heritage.

Mennonite communities were founded in both the United States and Canada, principally by German immigrants from the Rhine Valley. Their ancestors, who were persecuted for their opposition to infant baptism (they were called Anabaptists) and to the unity of church and state, left their native Switzerland during the Reformation era. Seeking greater freedom of worship, they emigrated from Germany to the New World. The Amish, who settled widely in eastern Pennsylvania, were Mennonite separatists who conducted their services in their homes. Other Mennonites built plain meetinghouses that reflected their hard-working, cooperative way of life. They interacted with the larger community through such enterprises as carriage building, and the remains of a Mennonite buggy factory may be seen in Elmira, Ontario, where the German immigrants were highly respected for their industrious ways as craftsmen and farmers.

The photographs that follow provide a panoramic view of the many faith communities that were established across the continent and the places of worship that housed their rites and strengthened their relationships. These modest churches have made an indelible imprint upon North American history and culture, although many of them have fallen into disuse or been replaced by grander structures serving larger, still active, congregations.

North American Gothic

On the previous pages is a community church in Standard, Vermont, with a late nineteenth-century belfry of patterned shinglework. Below, a pattern-book frame church in remote Hedley, British Columbia, seems dwarfed by the vast landscape. At right is a rural sanctuary with a short frontal tower in Chinook, Washington, a region of farms and ranches.

Signs of the Times

The Victorian love affair with the picturesque reached North America in the 1840s, as seen in these examples. On the opposite page is Trinity Church, Newfoundland, with attractive detailing and a free-standing bell tower. The weathered church above stands like a lonely sentinel on Fogo Island in Atlantic Canada.

For Generations to Come

The community church above, in Tennant, New Jersey, has ministered to its congregation since 1751—some twenty-five years before the American Revolution. On the opposite page (top) is Maine's historic Spurwink Church, established in 1802. Northwestern pioneers built the military chapel shown (below) at Fort Casey in Port Townsend, Washington.

A Place Apart

The Lutheran community built the distinctive sanctuary above, in Esofea, Wisconsin, in 1859. It was modified later in the century. Opposite, top, is the United Methodist Church in Thomaston, Maine; and below, charming St. Stephen's Episcopal Church (1841) in Millidgeville, Georgia.

Distinctive Masonry Churches

The serene fieldstone church at right, with red and white detailing, served as a schoolhouse in Soleberry, Pennsylvania, before it became St. Philip's Episcopal Chapel. Below is the Unitarian Universalist Church in Chester Depot, Vermont, built in 1845. Note the distinctive belfry, crowned with finials.

French and Spanish Influences

Unlike the Pilgrims and Puritans, who came to the New World to escape persecution for their religious beliefs, Roman Catholic missionaries from Spain and France came to propagate their faith among the native peoples. In fact, they participated in establishing the first permanent settlements in North America: the French at Quebec City (1608) and the Spanish at St. Augustine, Florida, in 1565. Most of these priests and friars, who were soon followed by dedicated women of religious orders, were deeply committed to their work and endured great hardships, including torture and martyrdom, to bring the Christian faith to Native Americans.

The expression "God, gold and glory" has become a byword for Spanish objectives in the New World, and notorious abuses were perpetrated by the conquistadors, but the Franciscan missionaries who accompanied them were sincere in their efforts to glorify God by preaching the faith and ministering to the native peoples. Initially, they sought to enrich others through spiritual values rather than to acquire wealth for themselves. Although this situation would change for the worse with the ascendance of the Spanish missions to worldly power, the original motive had been conversion, however misguided it may now appear to historians of the clash of cultures in the New World.

French and Spanish influences on church architecture are most apparent in Canada and the Mississippi Valley, and Florida and the Southwest, respectively. Few of the original French mission buildings—log constructions surrounded by palisades—have survived. For example, the Jesuits, called "Black Robes" by the Canadian tribes, established the mission of Ste. Marie for the Huron in 1639 near what is now Midland, Ontario. Founders Jean de Brebeuf and Gabriel Lalemont, with their associates,

Opposite: *San Francisco de Asis Church (1710), Ranchos de Taos, New Mexico.*

Below: *Chapel of San Miguel (c. 1640), Santa Fe.*

Opposite: *Above, Laurel Hill Church, in Adams County, Mississippi; below, the Church of the Holy Trinity (1847), Toronto, which features decorative quatrefoil tracery in the gable window.*

Below: *The Basilica of Notre Dame (1829) in Montreal, with twin towers and ornamentation in the French Gothic mode.*

preached and farmed there for ten years before the outpost was destroyed by the Huron and the missionaries killed. Fortunately, the old mission has been rebuilt in this century, adhering to using the methods of seventeenth-century France, to preserve this important segment of Canadian history. The French Jesuits extended their efforts as far south as present-day Auriesville, New York, where the Shrine of the North American Martyrs memorializes the death of Isaac Jogues and his companions at the hands of the Mohawk. In the course of evangelizing among the Mohawk, Father Jogues had penetrated some thousand miles inland, to the eastern entrance of Lake Superior, becoming the first European to reach this region.

In the cities of Quebec and Montreal (founded 1642), more imposing churches were soon built in the late-medieval tradition of northern France. Stone construction was reserved, at first, for permanent buildings including churches and seminaries, which confirmed that French settlers had come to stay (New France became a crown colony in 1663). Quebec City's Notre-Dame-des-Victoires, founded in 1688, has undergone many changes, but the original building was of fieldstone construction, plastered over for weatherproofing, with cut-stone trim around the doors and windows. Some Quebec-style churches have lateral transepts, which intersect the nave to make the cruciform plan characteristic of Christian ecclesiastical architecture. Many have round or squared apses—domed projections at the altar, or east, end, which traditionally faces toward Jerusalem. These sacred spaces were designed to awe and inspire, like the medieval cathedral. The bell tower, or *clocher*, often appears over the main façade at the apex of the roof. In more elaborate churches, twin spires flank the façade.

Montreal's Notre-Dame-de-Bon-Secours, begun in 1657 under the auspices of Marguerite Bourgeoys, foundress of the religious order the Congregation of Notre-Dame, was originally a modest wooden structure. Later it was rebuilt in stone, and many alterations occurred over time. The present structure dates from the late nineteenth century, with ceiling frescoes (recently restored) by painter Edouard Meloche depicting the life of the Virgin Mary. Her role as the protectress of travelers on the sea is symbolized by the great rooftop statue with arms outstretched toward the St. Lawrence, gateway to the city. Votive offerings in the form of model ships hang from the ceiling, given by sailors in gratitude for safe voyages.

Britain acquired Acadia (later Nova Scotia) in 1717 and deported all of its French colonists, many to the Mississippi River valley as far south as New Orleans and the bayou country around it. The Cajuns, as they would be called, built modest churches in the French vernacular style. Priests from Quebec had settled the area that is

now St. Louis, Missouri, as early as 1699, and by the early nineteenth century the city's large Catholic population was building its own cathedral, named for the French monarch and saint Louis IX. Constructed of polished sandstone, with a projecting Doric portico, the Old Cathedral, as it is now called, was elevated to the rank of Basilica of St. Louis the King in 1961.

New Orleans, too, built a parish church named for St. Louis the King, which served French Catholics from 1727 onward. In 1850 the present cathedral—the third church on this site, in the French Quarter's Jackson Square—was designed by the French architect J.N.B. DePouilly with triple spires and a conventional basilican plan. After the Louisiana Purchase of 1803, the city's English-speaking population increased and eventually built its own church, St. Patrick's, in 1833.

Atlantic Canada's population grew steadily under British rule (from 1763), and was increased by emigration from the New England colonies during and after the Revolutionary War. The classical Palladian style imported from the British Isles and the new United States affected Canadian church architecture throughout the nineteenth century. Masonry churches and cathedrals, both Anglican and Roman Catholic, were modeled upon those of the London architect James Gibbs, particularly St. Martin-in-the-Fields. The classical style was scaled down and interpreted in wood for small churches throughout eastern Canada. At the same time, the early Gothic Revival style found many adherents, and by the 1850s, Canadian architects were designing churches with irregular rooflines comprising towers and spires similar to those of French medieval cathedrals. As in the United States, many picturesque revival styles succeeded one another: Neoclassical, Italianate, Romanesque, Chateauesque. According to the authors of *A Guide to Canadian Architectural Styles* (Maitland et al., Broadview Press, 1992): "The use of Gothic Revival detail in a strictly decorative manner was never entirely abandoned, even when more historically correct tastes [including the Ecclesiological and High

Above: *St. Charles Borromeo Mission Church (1770), in Carmel, California, shows the influence of the Spanish Baroque style. Note that the right-hand bell tower was never finished with a dome like its counterpart.*

Victorian Gothic Revival styles] later appeared. These buildings have the symmetry and proportions of classicism with the details of the Gothic Revival, and as a body they constitute a readily recognizable vernacular type found throughout the country."

Roman and Moorish conquerors had brought the arch to Spanish architecture by the early eighth century, and with the "discovery" of the Americas in 1492, this architectural form made its way to the New World. The first Spanish chapel in the present-day United States was built at St. Augustine, Florida, where the parish of St. Augustine was established in 1593. Plans for a larger church were drawn up, but European wars and constant conflict between the Spanish settlers and the local native peoples whom they wished to Christianize delayed its completion for several centuries. The Cathedral of St. Augustine was not finished until 1870, and it was gutted by fire only seventeen years later. The present structure, enlarged and partially restored by the renowned architect James Renwick, retains only the façade and some of the side walls of the original building.

Spain's colonial empire in Mexico, which included most of what is now the American Southwest, had a decisive effect on regional architecture. Three of the Franciscan friars who accompanied Francisco de Coronado remained in New Mexico after 1540 to found a series of missions, the oldest of which is at Acoma Pueblo. Originally built in 1627, it combines Pueblo and Spanish-vernacular building techniques of adobe clay and brick with timber framing. Like other mission churches in New Mexico, Texas and California, Acoma Pueblo has relatively few windows and thick adobe walls to provide shelter from glaring sunlight and heat.

As historian Roger Kennedy observes in *American Churches* (Stewart, Tabori & Chang, 1982): "Stylistically, the twin towers and massive façades of mission churches, unornamented except about the doors and windows, seem to present a kind of provincial Baroque. Their spaces...feel as if they were Gothic, and their west façades feel like stern 'westworks' of the Romanesque—those great fortresses behind which the church itself extended itself warily in times of peace....The placement of [interior] light on figures of the Virgin or Christ, saints or martyrs, is intended to draw the eye upward, as it is in the much older Byzantine and Romanesque structures."

Mission San Jose y San Miguel de Aquayo, near San Antonio, Texas, was built by the Franciscans in the late 1700s and differs from most mission churches in being constructed of rough tufa (porous limestone) surfaced with stucco. It forms a large enclosed quadrangle and has a unique two-storied sculptured doorway depicting the Virgin surrounded by angels and saints. Only one of the two flanking towers was completed and serves as the belfry. The structure was falling into ruin by the early 1900s, but a concerted effort by civic and religious organizations restored it: now it is an active parish church. Another famous Texas mission church is the Alamo at San Antonio, founded in 1716. However, it was secularized in 1793 and joined with nearby settlements to form the provincial capital of San Antonio de Bexar. The old building was long deserted by the time it became the scene of the famous battle between American defenders and the Mexican army of General António López de Santa Anna in 1836.

In 1769 Father Junipero Serra established the first of twenty-one Franciscan missions in California—San Diego de Alcala, near what is now the city of San Diego. Among the best known of this chain of missions are San Luis Obispo de Tolosa (1772), San Francisco de Asis and San Juan Capistrano (both 1776), Santa Barbara (1786), and San Fernando Rey de España (1797), all of which gave their names to major California cities. The missions were secularized after the Republic of Mexico was established in 1810, but many of the old churches have been restored, including La Purísima Concepción, founded in 1787. It differs from most in having a linear rather than a quadrangular form, comprising a cemetery and adjoining church adjacent to living quarters, workshops and warehouses that once served as home to more than a thousand people. The enduring influence of Hispanic architecture has extended far beyond Florida and the Southwest, most recently in the Mission Revival style of the early 1900s, which brought red-roofed, adobe-style structures with patios and courtyards to cities and towns throughout the United States.

Below: *The restored mission of San Luis Obispo de Tolosa (1772), named for the Spanish bishop of Tolosa, is one of the chain of twenty-one California missions founded by the Franciscan Junipero Serra.*

Gothic-style Parish Churches

Graceful wooden churches with Gothic Revival detailing appeared in Atlantic Canada and New England in the early 1800s. On the opposite page is St. Francis of Assisi in Belfast, Maine, with a staged steeple and hooded pointed windows on the frontal tower and main building.

Vertical clapboard sheathing, a multilevel roofline and cross-shaped finials distinguish the handsome Anglican church at Peggy's Cove, Nova Scotia, below. The bell tower, with its French-style conical flared roof, is adjacent to the building and adds to its picturesque asymmetry.

Northeastern Masonry Churches

The sturdy fieldstone Anglican church at right, dedicated to St. James the Apostle, is in Lower Jemseg, New Brunswick. Its Gothic detailing contrasts with the Romanesque Revival elements of St. Saviour's Episcopal Church in Bar Harbor, Maine, below (1876). St. Saviour's massive, hip-roofed tower, broad eaves over a band of clerestory windows and stone columns flanking the entryway are typical of this period. Bar Harbor became a fashionable resort during the nineteenth century, 200 years after French Canada yielded its claim to Maine.

French Gothic Inspiration *overleaf*
The distinctive Gothic style of northern France is imprinted on the soaring Heinz Memorial Chapel (left), in Pittsburgh, Pennsylvania, and on the city's elegant St. Paul's Cathedral, (right). Hallmarks of the style include slender buttresses, triple portals, twin towers and great traceried windows filled with stained glass.

Pueblo-style Missions

Massive adobe-and-timber construction based on Native American architecture predominates in New Mexico, the first area of Franciscan evangelization in the Southwest. Opposite, below, are the ruins of the mission church built in 1717 at Pecos, which now form part of the Pecos National Monument. Above is El Santuario de Nuestro Señor de Esquipulas, more commonly known as the Santuario de Chimayo (1816), which has an enclosed courtyard and twin belfries that demonstrate the influence of Anglo settlement. Visitors today flock to the village of Chimayo in hopes of being restored by the miraculous healing powers that are attributed to this beautiful, serene shrine.

Texas and California Landmarks

Above is the handsome masonry church of San Francisco de Espada, built in what is now San Antonio, Texas, in 1731. Note the triple belfry, seen also on the Spanish Colonial church at right: Santa Inez, in Solvang, California. Opposite, top, is a building writ large in American history— the Alamo, originally the mission church of San Antonio de Valero, established in 1716. It had been secularized before it became the scene of battle between American and Mexican forces in 1836.

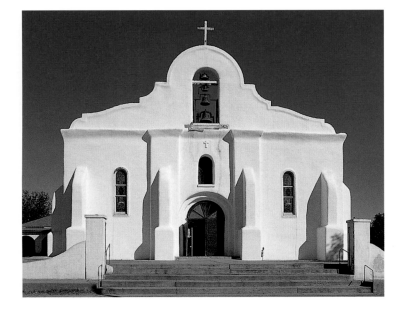

Studies in Light and Shadow

Many of the mission churches were whitewashed to reflect the harsh glare of the desert sun. The example above is the serene Chapel of San Elizario, at the Presidio in El Paso, Texas. At right, the intersection of Pueblo and Hispanic cultures is seen clearly in the mission complex at Taos, New Mexico, where Spanish Baroque forms combine with native materials and images to create a harmonious synthesis.

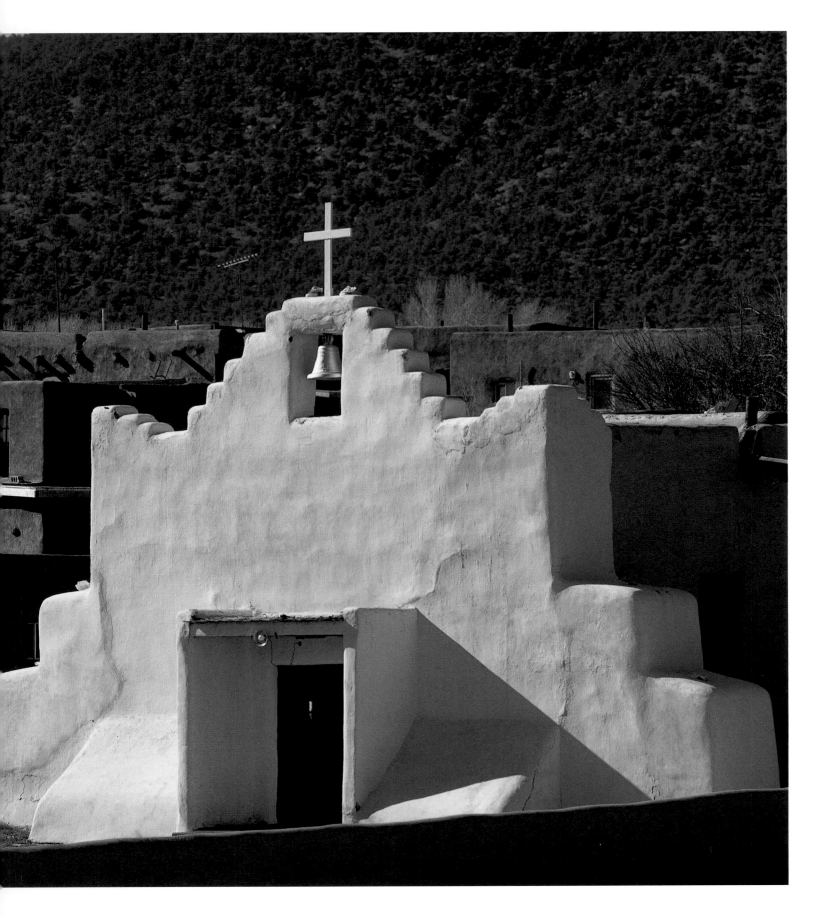

Southwest to Northeast

The arches and bell towers of the Iberian Peninsula were reprised wherever its emigrants built their churches in the New World. On the opposite page is the colonial church of San Felipe de Neri (1793), in Albuquerque. It is predated by New Mexico's San Miguel Mission church (above, 1620), now restored and modified for a new generation. At right is the Church of Our Lady of Good Voyage, built by a Portuguese fishing community in Gloucester, Massachusetts, in the early 1900s.

Greek and Gothic Revivals

During the nineteenth century, these contrasting styles had an overwhelming influence on North American architecture, as seen in churches, public buildings and houses all over the continent. The Greek Revival style became especially popular in the newly created United States, as an exemplar of the democratic and republican ideals enunciated by the Founding Fathers. It was also stimulated by new knowledge about classical antiquity acquired through Old World archaeological studies in Greece, as published in such books as *Antiquities of Athens* (1762), by British archaeologists James Stewart and N. Revett. Roman models, derived in part from Greek architecture, were also investigated, notably at Pompeii and Herculaneum, and Greco-Roman forms were combined, as in Jeffersonian Classicism. In fact, architecture was perhaps the United States' first contribution to art, in the form of such buildings as Thomas Jefferson's Virginia State Capitol at Richmond (1785), inspired by the monumental Roman temple with its domed rotunda.

The first Greek Revival building in the United States was not a church, but a commercial building in Philadelphia: the Bank of Pennsylvania, designed by British-American architect Benjamin Latrobe (1801). He collaborated with Jefferson on the conversion of Monticello, originally a Georgian mansion, to the new classical style and designed the Cathedral of the Assumption in Baltimore, Maryland (1818), widely considered the best use of the Greek Revival in any American building. His other

notable churches include Christ Church (1805) and St. John's (1816), both in Washington, D.C. At Jefferson's behest, Latrobe made major contributions to the construction of the U.S. Capitol building and the White House, to which he added terraced pavilions and porticoes. It was the new national capital that gave the greatest impetus to the emergent Greek Revival style, which had traveled as far west as San Francisco by 1850, attendant upon the Gold Rush.

Latrobe trained two great American architects who would become notable church designers—Robert Mills and William Strickland. Mills's buildings were simple and bold, as seen

Opposite: *The historic First Church of Quincy, Massachusetts (1828), the Greek Revival-style parish church attended by Presidents John Adams and John Quincy Adams.*

Below: *St. Luke's Church is a picturesque Carpenter Gothic landmark in Clermont, New York.*

Right: *The old meetinghouse in Royalton, Vermont, was refurbished in the early 1800s with the newly fashionable pediment and pilasters of the Greek Revival.*

in Washington, D.C.'s, National Portrait Gallery (1840), originally the U.S. Patent Office. His first major ecclesiastical commissions were in Philadelphia, for the Sansom Street Baptist Church (1809) and the Octagon Unitarian Church (1813). His competition-winning design for Richmond's Monumental Church (1812), a memorial to seventy-one victims of a fire, incorporated a stone porch of Doric inspiration, square in plan, and an octagonal main building of brick and stucco with a low dome.

Like his mentor Latrobe, William Strickland combined the skills of architectural design, engineering and construction. The son of a master carpenter, he set up his own practice in his native Philadelphia at the age of twenty. In 1828 he restored the city's historic Independence Hall and added the present steeple. After moving south to Nashville, Tennessee, to design the state's capitol building, he constructed several churches, notably the Old First Presbyterian Church (1851), a departure into the exotic Egyptian Revival style, which was also inspired by archaeological discoveries, including the Temple at Karnak on the Nile.

Professional architects were the first to build churches in the Greek-temple mode, but builders and carpenters learned to emulate the style through manuals and pattern books. They mas-

tered the intricacies of the classical Greek orders, beginning with the Doric, as exemplified by the Parthenon at Athens (432 BC) and developed later by the Romans, who added a molded base at the foot of the column. The Ionic order originated in Asia Minor, with larger volutes (fluted patterning) on the column and a scrolled capital, or head, supporting the architrave. The Corinthian order, with a still more intricate capital of botanical inspiration, appeared on the Temple of Jupiter at Athens about AD 50.

It was not easy to make a small wooden church look like a solid-stone temple, but vernacular examples nationwide show how these designs were adapted to houses of worship in many different faith communities, often by adding a simple portico to an existing building. A number of New England meetinghouses were altered in this way during the early nineteenth century, as seen in the First Church of Templeton, Massachusetts (1811), and Meriden, Connecticut's, Center Church (1830). It can be difficult to distinguish these buildings from earlier churches in the Georgian and Federal styles, with their classical detailing. However, there are several telling differences. The Greek Revival church generally has a flatter roof, on which the steeple, in several squared stages, is set back. The dominant columned portico, usually in the Doric mode, extends the full width of the façade. Masonry construction also became more prevalent, as seen in the First Church of Quincy, Massachusetts, known as the Stone Temple. Designed by architect Alexander Parris, it was built in 1828 of granite presented to the parish by President John Adams. He and his son, President John Quincy Adams, are buried here.

In Canada, the Greek Revival of the United States had its counterpart in the Neoclassical style (1820s–50s), which also differed from Palladianism in several ways, principally in the use of details taken directly from ancient Greek and Roman prototypes, rather than from Renaissance models. Design became more linear, with untextured façades free of prominent moldings. Both Greek and Roman columns appeared, modeled principally on the Ionic and Doric orders, and detailing included acanthus leaves and Greek fretwork and key designs. A handsome example of the style is Saint-Grégoire (1850) in Nicolet, Quebec, by architect Augustin Leblanc. It has low flanking towers, arched bays and harmonious stonework from portico to pediment.

Growing interest in the picturesque was reflected from about 1840 in the Early Gothic Revival, especially apparent in ecclesiastical architecture. Inspired by the writings of English cultural historians John Ruskin and Augustus Pugin, both American and Canadian architects began to design churches based upon the Gothic style of the Middle Ages, manifested in various modes throughout western Europe. The first major Gothic Revival church in the United States was New York City's Trinity Church (1846), designed by Richard Upjohn. Its soaring ornamental form was widely admired, and by 1860 Upjohn had published a book of plans for modest wooden Gothic churches in country and small-town locations entitled *Rural Church Architecture*.

Another pioneer of the style was James Renwick, Jr., whose landmarks include New York City's Grace Church (1845), Riverdale Presbyterian (1863) and St. Patrick's Cathedral, designed in the 1850s in the spirit of Germany's twin-spired Cathedral of Cologne. Under construction for thirty years, it became a symbol of the emergent Irish-American Catholic community, which started out as a disparaged minority during the wave of immigration that followed the devastating famine known as "the Great Hunger," caused by the blight of Ireland's staple potato crop. St. Patrick's departed from the Anglican/Episcopal tradition of a single frontal tower, but its interior is in the beautiful English style, with decorative lath-and-plaster vaulting rather than heavy stonework. New York's Episcopalians immediately sought to build something still grander in the form of the Cathedral Church of St. John the Divine (begun 1893), which combines Romanesque and High Victorian Gothic forms.

In the eclectic way of Victorian architecture, the High Victorian Gothic style was based largely on medieval examples from northern Italy, rather than England or France. Popularized by John Ruskin's books *The Seven Lamps of Architecture* (1849) and *The Stones of Venice*

Below: *The Greek Revival reached California during the Gold Rush of the late 1840s, as seen in the First Methodist Church of Eureka.*

(1851–53), the style has also been called Ruskinian Gothic and is characterized by the use of polychrome (multicolored) stone, bricks and slate that make color and pattern integral to the building. One example of the style, which flourished nationwide during the late nineteenth century, is the Camillus Baptist Church in Camillus, New York, by architect Archimedes Russell (1880). It has a steep gabled roof and projecting side porches, both roofed with bands of slate tiles in different colors and patterns. Its narrow offset tower is crowned by a spire that flares at the eaves, topped by a finial. Smooth board siding gives this frame church the appearance of stonework.

The American master of the High Victorian Gothic style was Philadelphia architect Frank Furness, perhaps best known for his outstanding Pennsylvania Academy of Art, in his home city (1876). Unfortunately, few of his notable churches have survived, apart from the First Unitarian Church of Philadelphia (1886), designed for his father's former parish. Architect Alexander Jackson Davis, who did more than anyone else to popularize the Gothic Revival in the United States, designed several churches in 1838, including the Dutch Reformed Church in Newburgh, New York, and the First Unitarian Church in New Bedford, Massachusetts. However, most of his work was residential.

Among the continent's most appealing Gothic-style churches are the countless vernacular buildings designed and constructed by their own congregations, many of which appear in the plates that follow. Their dignity, simplicity and craftsmanship have made them cherished landmarks in communities from Newfoundland and Nova Scotia to the Far West. Many were built in the inexpensive Carpenter Gothic style, with vertical board-and-batten sheathing and diamond-paned lancet windows. Others resemble small frame houses, with pointed doors and windows and perhaps a modest cupola-style belfry to identify them as places of worship. The parishioner of one such church, Larry Hutson, recalled its origins in southwestern Wisconsin for *Country Magazine* (Feb/Mar 1999):

"Big Creek United Methodist Church sits just a quarter mile away from the creek that gave the valley its name....The simple structure was built in 1874 with lumber purchased from a sawmill in Tomah at a cost of $9 per thousand board feet. Church members made the 20-mile trip to pick up the lumber in horse-drawn wagons—leaving at 4 AM in minus-30-degree weather....We held church socials in the old horse shed after it had outlived its usefulness for that purpose."

Recollections like these are a valuable contribution to our oral history at a time when many old churches have been pulled down, closed up, or converted to other uses. Fortunately, many others have survived to attest to the deep faith of our forefathers and -mothers, who brought their beliefs to the New World and built sacred places across the continent in which to share and strengthen their relationships with God and one another.

On the Village Green

After the Revolutionary War, New Englanders adopted the pillared porticoes of the Greek Revival, which were often added to colonial meetinghouses. On the opposite page is the Congregational Church at Bar Harbor, Maine, with a set-back steeple to accommodate the full-width Greek façade. Above, the First Congregational Church of Norwalk, Connecticut; at right, Washington, Connecticut's, First Congregational Church (1801).

Town and Country

Affluent congregations commissioned professional architects to design their houses of worship. On the opposite page is Massachusetts' beautiful First Church of Christ (Lancaster Meetinghouse) by Boston architect Charles Bulfinch (1817), which some consider his masterwork. Left, the elegant First Baptist Church in Galveston, Texas, epitomizes the Greek Revival style. Below is New York City's eclectic Church of St. Paul the Apostle, with circular windows and a niche for its patron saint in the pediment.

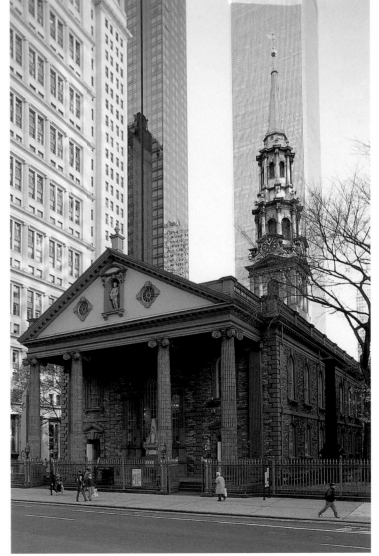

Stylistic Combinations

Kirtland Temple in Kirtland, Ohio, at right, was the first Mormon temple in the United States built to founder Joseph Smith's specifications in an eclectic style that combined Federal, Greek and Gothic elements (1836). On the opposite page is St. Augustine's Roman Catholic Church in Philadelphia, Pennsylvania, with rounded Palladian windows, a Greek cornice and ornamental quoins (patterned stonework) on the frontal tower. The prosperity of pre-Civil War Natchez, Mississippi, is reflected in the city's classical First Presbyterian Church, below, built in 1828. On the following pages, a vernacular frame church in remote New Bonaventure, Newfoundland.

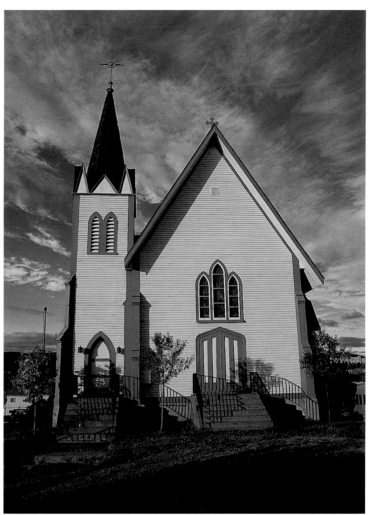

Atlantic Canadian Gothic

Skilled woodworkers built both of these delightful community churches. At left is a shingled and painted church on St. Peter's Bay, Prince Edward Island. It has a frontal tower crowned by a conical spire with flared eaves and louvered windows. Above, an offset side tower with its own entrance distinguishes the Anglican church at Edmundston, New Brunswick, with its steeply sloped roof.

From New England to the Northwest

During the nineteenth century, the Gothic Revival became the foremost style in church architecture, as seen from these examples spanning the continent. The church below is preserved at Minnesota's Pioneer Village. At right is the Mendocino (California) Presbyterian Church (1859), and below it, Trinity Lutheran Church in Washington Depot, Connecticut.

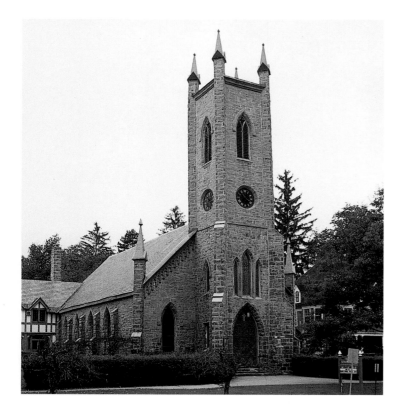

Brick and Stone Construction

In keeping with the original Gothic mode of building in masonry, many community churches used durable materials to good effect. On the opposite page is St. Patrick's in New Castle, Maine (1808). At left is St. James Church in Sheffield, Massachusetts (1857); below, the eclectic Methodist Church of Rhinebeck, New York.

Landmark Spires

On the opposite page is New York City's venerable
Trinity Church (1846), which served Manhattan's first
Episcopalian parish. It was designed by architect Richard
Upjohn, with sculptured bronze doors by Richard Morris
Hunt. At right is the well-proportioned Gothic church
of the Holy Trinity, in coastal Westport, Connecticut.
A wide Midwestern sky frames the lovely rural church below,
in Old Mendota, Minnesota.

Late Victorian Gothic

Elaborate ornamentation appeared in the eclectic Gothic churches built before and after the turn of the century. On the opposite page is flamboyant St. John Cathedral, inspired by Dutch and Flemish medieval styles, in Lafayette, Louisiana. The Red Hook, New York, church at right has vertical board-and-batten cladding and an unusual Stick-style belfry that contributes to the vertical thrust of the building. Below, the United Church of Randolph, Vermont, with Eastlake-style detailing in gables, towers and window surrounds.

Romanesque and Eclectic Victorian Styles

Romanesque architecture originally flourished in western Europe until about the twelfth century, when it was superseded by the Gothic style, which incorporated many of its principles. The style was based largely on Roman prototypes, but Byzantine and other elements also played a part in it. As Christianity spread through the known world, churches in the Romanesque mode often rose on the sites of former pagan temples. Built mainly of stone, they incorporated the Roman system of semicircular, or barrel, vaulting, but evolved a method of ribbed vaulting to replace the heavy stone groins where vaults crossed one another. Chunky towers, short buttresses and domed apses were characteristic features of the style.

During the early nineteenth century, several Canadian and American architects took up the Romanesque style and adapted it for churches and other public buildings of their own time. In Canada, the English or Norman Romanesque style gained favor, as seen in brick or stone churches with projecting square towers; round-arched entryways with bands of stylized decoration; and tiers of arched windows that varied in size and treatment, from single to triple groupings.

A Germanic version of the style, based on Italian models, occurs in the Roman Catholic Basilica of St. John the Baptist (begun 1845) in St. John's, Newfoundland, with square towers capped by hip roofs. Several handsome buildings of native limestone were built in the Norman style in Montreal, including

St. Brigide's Church, designed by architects Martin, de Potras and Martin (1878). It has a prominent frontal tower (with a steeple added later) and typical arched openings and corner buttresses.

Opposite: *St. Peter's by the Sea (Stick style, 1876), Cape May, New Jersey.*

Above: *A short, blocky tower and polychrome stonework and shingling distinguish the Romanesque/Gothic Trinity Episcopal Church in Lime Rock, Connecticut.*

Previous Page: *Portland, Maine's, First Parish Meetinghouse (1825–26) is of masonry construction and features a Romanesque tower and three-bay façade.*

In the United States, architect Henry Hobson Richardson (1838–86) was the pre-eminent practitioner of Romanesque Revival architecture—to the degree that the unique American version of the style is often called Richardsonian Romanesque. Although he lived for less than fifty years and designed fewer than one hundred buildings, Richardson's reputation was high in his lifetime and has increased since his death.

Richardson was born into a prosperous Louisiana family and studied at what is now Tulane University, New Orleans, and Harvard University. In 1860 he became the second American to be admitted to the prestigious *École des Beaux Arts* in Paris. After returning to the United States, he practiced architecture in New York City and Boston, where he created increasingly beautiful buildings inspired by traditional forms interpreted in his own creative style. His earliest major commissions were for two Massachusetts churches that he designed in the High Victorian style, both in 1869. His own powerful Romanesque style appeared in the imposing Brattle Square Church, Boston, in

1872. Still more massive elements in the form of low arches, rounded forms and a conical roofline were used for the Emmanuel Episcopal Church in Pittsburgh, Pennsylvania (1886).

By general agreement, Richardson's masterwork is Boston's Trinity Church, built between 1872 and 1877 on Copley Square. His competition-winning design for this landmark Episcopal church called for rough Dedham granite with Longmeadow sandstone trim. French Romanesque influence is paramount in the opulent polychrome structure, which features stained-glass windows by John La Farge, William Morris and Edward Burne-Jones. Richardson's peers in architecture voted Trinity Church America's best building in 1885. When the architect was buried from Trinity Church in 1886, its rector, Phillips Brooks, said in his eulogy: "Whoever came in contact with his works felt that the wind blew out of an elemental simplicity, out of the primitive life and qualities of man....It was that which made his work delightful."

Several other American designers made impressive use of Romanesque Revival forms during the late nineteenth century. They included William A. Potter, who designed the Episcopal church of St. Mary's-in-Tuxedo (1888) for the fashionable resort of Tuxedo Park, New York. It combines rusticated masonry, shinglework and steeply gabled rooflines with eclectic Victorian ornamentation.

Chicago architect Daniel Burnham was an admirer of Richardson's work, whose influence is seen in St. Gabriel's Church in Chicago (1887), by Burnham and his partner John Wellbron Root. For some time, Root also worked with James Renwick, Jr., who designed the original Smithsonian Institution building in Washington, D.C. (1849). In partnership with Joseph Sands, Renwick also designed New York City's St. Ann's Church (1867) in the High Victorian Gothic style.

The burgeoning West Coast showed its new ethnic diversity and prosperity in many church buildings that rose in the late 1800s. In Los Angeles, California, which became accessible by railroad in 1881, there were so many sects that one observer wrote: "There are probably more religions in Los Angeles than in the whole previous history of mankind." The city's historic ties to Roman Catholicism remained strong, as seen in the construction of the Spanish Baroque Cathedral of St. Vibiania in 1876, but many exotic new structures were erected, including the First Hebrew Christian Church, with a large open scroll on its roof. San Francisco dedicated the church now known as Old St. Mary's Cathedral in 1854, and the First United Methodist Church of Salem, Oregon, was built in the High Victorian Gothic style in 1878.

Many other eclectic styles of the Victorian era also manifested themselves in church architecture, combining Gothic, vernacular, Italianate, Exotic, Beaux-Arts and other elements in response to the nineteenth-century resurgence in religion called "The Age of the Great Revival." Both evangelical and traditional churches—Methodist, Episcopal, Roman Catholic—experienced growth through conversion, immigration and a renewed focus on liturgy, as expressed in their respective houses of worship. Historian Roger Kennedy discusses the unprecedented growth of the evangelical denominations, especially the Methodist, as the hallmark of the period. In *American Churches*,

he states that: "We have good reason to use the term 'Great Revival' for this phenomenon, because it occurred most vehemently in the folded valleys of the Appalachians and in the great flat river basin west of those mountains. To focus attention there is useful because this may balance a picture that otherwise might be distorted by the persuasiveness of those Yankee historians who tend to depict American history as if it all occurred within easy commuting distance of Cambridge, Massachusetts."

A multitude of sects grew up during this period, many of them fostered by the pressing social and moral issues of the day, from slavery and temperance to missionary work at home and abroad. Traditional communities like the Lutherans divided along regional lines, as vexed issues polarized North and South and divided long-settled Easterners from westward migrants. Wealthy urban congregations enlarged or renovated their existing churches in fashionable styles, while poorer congregations sometimes became the beneficiaries of an outgrown or outmoded building given up by another denomination.

In the West, it was not uncommon, as mentioned in chapter 2, for several congregations to share worship space for economy and convenience. Even conservative New England diversified its church architecture in the wake of major

Left: *Christ Church Episcopal, with an unusual free-standing tower with battlements, in Canaan, Connecticut.*

Above: *The delightfully eclectic Baptist Church of Ludlow, Vermont, with its conical Chateauesque towers and Stick-style ornamentation, dates from the late nineteenth century.*

immigrations from Ireland, Italy and eastern Europe. New Canadian churches differed widely from eastern prototypes, as this vast land became more densely populated from the prairie provinces to affluent British Columbia. In the case of frontier churches, pattern books and manuals continued to help neophyte church builders, with Richard Upjohn's *Rural Architecture* perhaps the most influential.

An interesting case study in nineteenth-century architectural changes is that of St. Peter's Church on Capitol Hill, in Washington, D.C. The second Roman Catholic church in the capital, it was designed in the classical style by architect James Hoban and dedicated in 1821. In 1888 a new and larger church in the Romanesque style, with Gothic elements, was designed to serve the growing parish. This building stood until well into the twentieth century, and when it was partially destroyed by fire, the exterior

walls and stained-glass windows were incorporated into the new structure. Wherever possible, faith communities tried to preserve the best of their existing churches when modifications became necessary.

Another distinguished eclectic Victorian church in the capital is Concordian United Church of Christ (1892), designed by architects Paul Schulze and Albert Goenner. Originally known as the Concordian Lutheran Evangelical Church, it is the third building on the site to serve a German congregation that was formed in the late eighteenth century. It combines Gothic Revival and German Baroque features, with stepped gables and a four-story tower on the northwest corner. Concordia shares stylistic elements with the German Gothic church of St. Mary's in the Mountains, in faraway Virginia City, Nevada.

Charleston, South Carolina, is the site of the New Tabernacle Fourth Baptist Church (1862), the achievement of architect Francis D. Lee. Originally built for an Episcopal congregation as St. Luke's, it is a large brick building in the shape of a Greek cross, with Gothic windows thirty-seven feet high and Tudor arches rising from the interior columns to the ceiling. Damaged by shells during the Civil War, it suffered further destruction in the 1880s from a hurricane and an earthquake. Fortunately, the historic building was purchased and restored by its new Baptist congregation in 1950 and has become a vital force in the city's spiritual life.

The New York City firm of Cram, Goodhue and Ferguson designed many notable churches at the turn of the century, most of them in the Eclectic Gothic style. Partner Ralph Adams Cram (1863–1943) brought in many commissions through his books and lectures, while others were obtained by means of competitions. Bertram Grosvenor Goodhue (1869–1924) was a talented designer, while Frank Ferguson was a gifted administrator and businessman. Among their best-known works are All Saints Church (1895), in Brookline, Massachusetts; St. Stephen's (1900), in Cohasset, Massachusetts; and New York City's St. Thomas's Episcopal Church (1914).

Beaux-Arts architect Richard Morris Hunt left his imprint on the influential World's Columbian Exposition at Chicago in 1893. Best known for his imposing mansions and such monumental buildings as New York City's Metropolitan Museum of Art, he designed the great bronze doors for Richard Upjohn's beautiful Trinity Church, at Wall Street and Broadway. His friend Karl T.F. Bitter, who sculpted the doors, placed Hunt's image on the frame of the right-hand door. A founder and third president of the American Institute of Architects, Hunt also designed the Vanderbilt Mausoleum (1886), which is in New York City's Moravian Cemetery.

In some cases, attractive Victorian ornamentation, including Stick-style and Eastlake detailing, were used to beautify a plain wooden structure, as seen in the following plates. Skilled masons learned the techniques of polychrome stone- and brickwork, and roofers laid shingles and tiles in the decorative bands of the Queen Anne Revival style. Four-square Romanesque towers were incorporated into Gothic Revival churches, and fanciful conical towers of French and German inspiration gave late-century churches a castle-like quality. Most nineteenth-century churches retained their adjacent cemeteries, but many had to purchase additional space at some distance to expand their burial grounds. The Gothic mode remained dominant in ecclesiastical architecture, but countless variations on this theme sprang up to lend distinction, grace and variety to parish churches across the continent.

Below: *The First Baptist Church of Macon, Georgia (1887), exemplifies the elaborate High Victorian Gothic style, which freely combined such elements as decorative brick and stonework, towers of unequal size and massive gable and eave trim.*

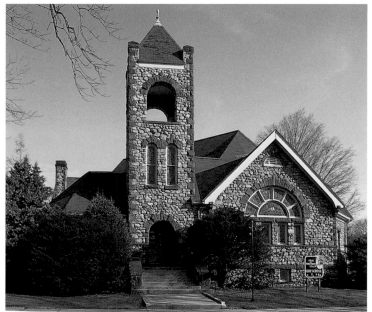

Romanesque Polychrome Masonry

Strong masonry construction and short, square towers define these late nineteenth-century churches in New York and New England. Above, Christ and Holy Trinity Church in coastal Westport, Connecticut, built of native stone and incorporating several arched openings. At left, All Saints Episcopal Church in Hoosick, New York, which features striking polychrome ornamentation and an unusual asymmetrical tower with attached corner steeple.

Richardsonian Romanesque

The unmistakable imprint of Henry Hobson Richardson is seen in the massing and details of these rusticated-stone churches, imbued with presence and power. The example above is the First Church Congregational in Fairfield, Connecticut. Opposite, top, is the chapel at the University of Virginia in Charlottesville, a campus designed by Thomas Jefferson. Opposite, below, St. Hugo's Church in Michigan.

Overleaf (left) is Henry Hobson Richardson's unique Trinity Church, Boston, the first full expression of his eponymous Romanesque style. Its polychrome stonework and central lantern-shaped tower (derived from the Cathedral of Salamanca) command historic Copley Square. At right is the roughly textured Bethel Mehodist Evangelical Church (1862), with contrasting stonework, in Hilda, Texas.

Victorian Spires

These eclectic late-Victorian churches show a variety of spires that add a strong vertical element to the composition. At left is the First Presbyterian Church of Port Wilson, Washington (1889). Queen Anne Revival influence is apparent in St. Mary's Church on Whidbey Island, Washington, below. On the opposite page, Gothic Revival and the indigenous Stick style join hands to graceful effect in St. John the Baptist Episcopal Church in Thomaston, Maine.

Asymmetrical Elegance

These eclectic houses of worship feature imposing square towers with contrasting spire and window styles. At left is the handsome, turn-of-the-century Cape Island Presbyterian Church in the resort of Cape May, New Jersey, a National Historic community. Below, left: Chappell Hill (Texas) United Methodist Church (1901) has a symmetrical façade up to the main roofline, but contrasting towers, the larger one housing the belfry. Below is the Anglican church of scenic Fogo, Newfoundland, which was built in the vernacular English Gothic style.

Rooflines and Detailing

A distinctive double gable with strong Eastlake ornamentation forms an inviting approach to St. Bridget Church (opposite) in charming Cornwall Bridge, Connecticut. At right, a picturesque church at Hunter River, on Prince Edward Island, features steeply sloping rooflines designed to shed snow. Below is the serene classical-cum-Gothic Clinton Presbyterian Church in New Jersey.

Gothic Triumphant

Nineteenth-century congregations favored the dominant vertical lines of the Gothic Revival style above all others, as seen on the opposite page at the Thomaston (Maine) Baptist Church, with its strong classical elements. The Bodega, California, church at left is a charming vernacular example, while the New England Presbyterian church below is a departure from the region's original Puritan style.

Apogee of the Eclectic

The High Victorian style took ornamentation to new heights, as seen on the opposite page in St. John's Anglican Church (top) at Trinity, Newfoundland, and St. Matthew Roman Catholic Church in Royalton, Vermont. Below, exterior banding, diverse window treatments and a Chateauesque tower with Gothic spire embellish St. Mary's Church at Indian River, Prince Edward Island.

Details and Ornamentation

Sacred art and architecture have inspired some of the most creative endeavors in human history, and our places of worship combine these works in countless ways. The diverse and powerful symbols of the Christian faith pervade these sanctuaries, speaking directly to the human spirit. Almost every aspect of church architecture expresses an attribute of the divine and of the relationship between a loving Creator and His offspring, as embodied in the only prayer taught by Christ to His disciples, which begins with the words "Our Father."

The cross, as the primary symbol of Christianity, is found in most churches and takes different forms based on ethnicity, culture and tradition. In Roman Catholicism, it is generally the crucifix, that is, a cross on which the body of Christ, or *corpus*, is depicted in the agony of His sacrificial death for humankind. Most of the Protestant faith communities use the simple Latin cross without the *corpus* as a sign of Christ's Resurrection—the central mystery of the faith. The Greek cross, often used for the plan of Orthodox churches, has four equal arms radiating from the center, while the Latin cross forms the cruciform church plan most familiar in Western Christianity, in which the transept crosses the nave, or central worship space. Irish immigrants introduced the familiar Celtic cross, with its circular surround.

North American churches draw mainly upon European prototypes for their design and decoration, including the basilica and Romanesque styles that evolved before about AD 1200 and the various Gothic styles of the Middle Ages, which drew upon these prototypes. The medieval cathedral, often built over centuries rather than years, symbolized aspiration of the highest kind, as seen in the soaring pinnacles and vaulted ceilings that seemed to unite earth and heaven in physical form, as Christ united both human and divine natures in the Incarnation. Because most early and medieval Christians were illiterate, it became customary to depict scenes from the

Opposite: *The monumental sculpture of Our Lady of Good Help by P. Laperce (1893) crowns the historic Chapel of Notre-Dame-de-Bon-Secours in Old Montreal. Her arms are outstretched toward the St. Lawrence River, gateway to the city.*

Left: *Intrinsic to the Christian tradition, angels are often depicted in sacred art and architecture as celestial guardians.*

Right: *Delicate metalwork ornamentation—hinges and studs—at the entrance to Pittsburgh's landmark Heinz Memorial Chapel.*

Right: *Delicate metalwork ornamentation—hinges and studs—at the entrance to Pittsburgh's landmark Heinz Memorial Chapel.*

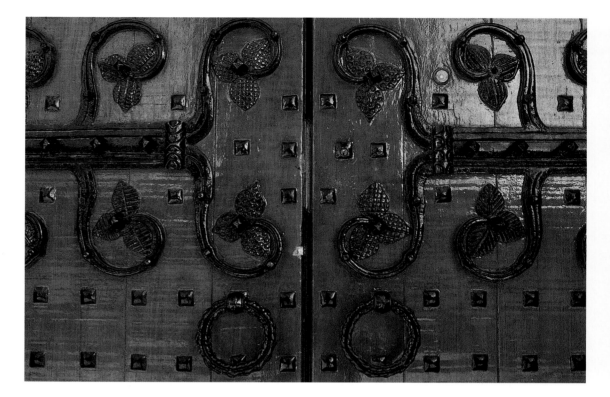

Right: *Winged angels, symbols of divine mission, were often used to decorate church exteriors.*

Gospels and the lives of the saints in stained-glass windows, murals, sculptures and reliefs, and this tradition has been retained for its beauty and power long after literacy became the norm in Western society. The Renaissance era made new use of classical forms that emphasized rich ornamentation, culminating in the Baroque styles of Spain, Germany and other European countries whose emigrants tried to replicate their familiar worship spaces in the New World.

The theme of light is represented not only in stained glass, but also in votive and altar candles, icon lamps, clerestories (bands of clear windows placed high in the walls) and marble or gilded columns and altars, which are sometimes inlaid with bright mosaics of glittering stone, as in the Byzantine tradition. Where the Lord's Supper, or holy communion in the form of bread and wine, forms part of the liturgy, chalices and patens, or plates, of precious metal embossed with symbolic designs have been used to consecrate and distribute the Eucharist (from the Greek word for thanksgiving). Where emphasis is placed on the word of God as proclaimed and preached upon from the scriptures, the pulpit is the focal point of the church. Often elaborately carved and ornamented, it stands above the congregation, much as the steeple crowns the building.

Bell towers are a major feature of Christian architecture, and have been erected in stone, brick, wood, adobe and other materials native to North America. They call people to worship, or to pause and pray, and their resonant music marks the great passages of life: confirmation in the faith, the sacrament of marriage, the sor-

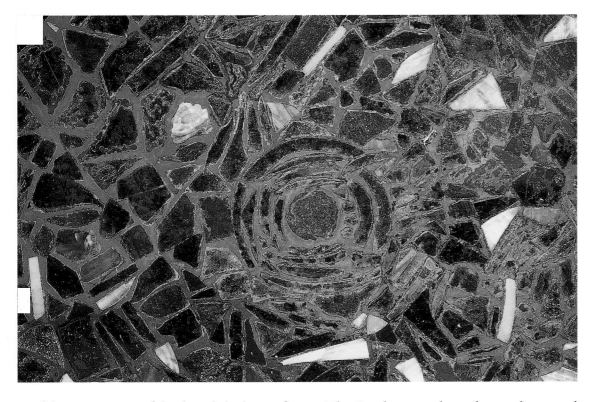

Left: *An intricate and richly colored design of a Byzantine-inspired mosaic from a chapel in Beaufort, South Carolina.*

rowful turning point of death and the hope of resurrection and eternal reunion.

Some of our most beautiful sanctuaries speak to simplicity rather than opulence, as seen in the uncluttered lines of historic New England churches, Quaker meetinghouses, Shaker communes, log mission chapels and frame structures built by the pioneers. What they lack in decoration, they make up in careful, craftsmanlike detailing—whether hand-carved sculptures, wrought metal hinges, bookstands, or pews and pulpits fashioned by local carpenters.

As precut lumber and machine tools became available during the nineteenth century, woodworkers used their skills to ornament their churches with turned spindlework, jig-sawn gingerbread trim, applied stickwork, patterned shingles and other embellishments. Almost the only Victorian style rarely used for church architecture was French Second Empire—not a revival style, but an introduction of the 1870s that was considered more suitable for residential and commercial buildings. The Shingle style, rooted in English colonial architecture and popularized by Henry Hobson Richardson for Eastern resorts, was adopted widely after the 1876 Centennial celebration, and shingle-clad churches were being built in the Midwest by the late nineteenth century.

The Southwest reclaimed its architectural heritage in the Pueblo, Mission and Spanish Colonial Revivals of the turn of the century, which featured flat or pyramidal red-tiled roofs, curvilinear gables with elaborately carved ornamentation, a patio or courtyard, and asymmetrically arranged rooms of varying size. Each ethnic and regional group brought its skills to bear in creating and re-creating churches that linked their congregations with hallowed traditions and, at the same time, looked forward to growth and expansion on behalf of their children and the generations to come after them.

Below: *Brickwork at the Church of Prince William's Parish, more commonly known as Old Sheldon Church, in Yemassee, South Carolina, is pockmarked by Civil War bullets. Built between 1745 and 1755, the church was burned by the British in 1779 and the Federal Army in 1865.*

Spanish Mission Churches

On the opposite page, the lavishly ornate Spanish Baroque entryway to San Antonio's San Jose Mission (1760), replete with images of the saints, scrollwork and botanical reliefs, also features an intricately carved front door. The unusual Albuquerque, New Mexico, church below combines typical Mission features, including its adobe wall, double frontal towers and walled courtyard, with Gothic Revival detailing, as seen in the louvered windows, pointed arches and finials on the towers.

Signs of Aspiration

Demonstrating the diversity of architectural interpretations of this feature is a selection of towers and spires symbolizing the union of heaven and earth. Clockwise from above: the quintessential New England spire of the New Preston Congregational Church, in New Preston, Connecticut; the awe-inspiring Gothic design of St. John's Cathedral, in Paterson, New Jersey; and the lavishly ornamented eclectic United Methodist Church of Litchfield (Connecticut), which combines Gothic, classical and Victorian elements.

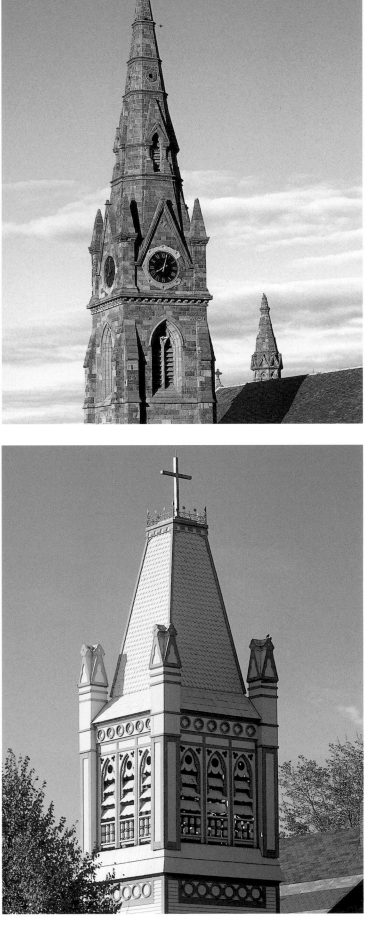

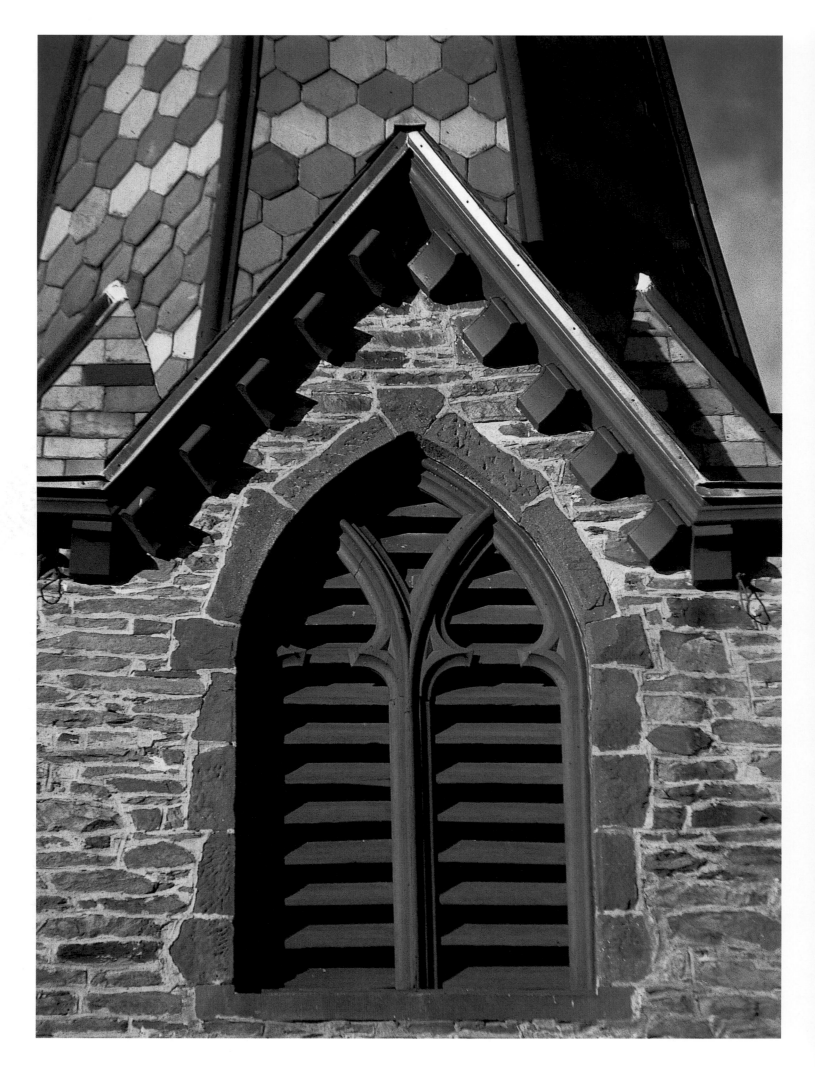

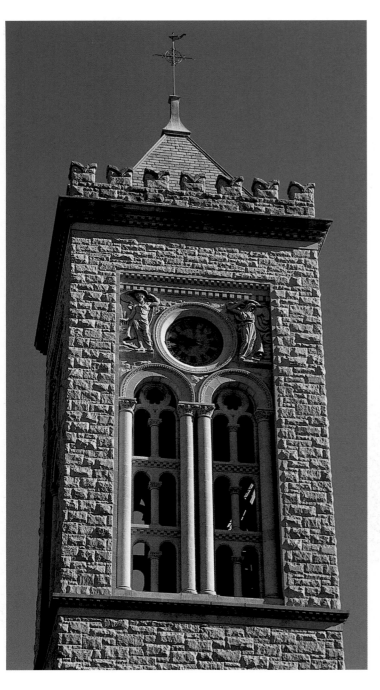

Changing Fenestration

Stained glass was incorporated into religious architecture to illuminate the interior space with a myriad of colors. Many featured scenes from the life of Christ, while others were more decorative. The rose, a common symbol of the Virgin Mary, was often used, as seen in the example below, which features a traceried rose window in handsome surrounds at St. John the Baptist Catholic Church, in Pittsburgh, Pennsylvania. A major distinction between the classical and Gothic styles was in fenestration—the design and placement of windows. At left, the eclectic tower of the Presbyterian Church (1893) in Morristown, New Jersey, features Palladian arched window openings. On the opposite page is a louvered Gothic window in the patterned steeple of St. Paul's Church (1868) in Tivoli, New York.

Founders of the Faith

A spectrum of sculptural icons from the Christian tradition, beginning with the rugged wooden crucifix at Clarkson Chapel, in Columbia County, New York (above); a gilded statue of the Madonna, with scepter and crown, and Child, whose arms are outstretched to the world, from the Chapel of Notre-Dame-de-Bon-Secours in Old Montreal (right). On the opposite page is a Canadian Gothic steeple encircled by saints at St. Mary's Church, in Prince Edward Island.

"Ye Watchers and Ye Holy Ones"

Sculptures and scenes from the Bible were often placed on the exteriors of churches to remind the worshipper of God's power. St. Michael the Archangel overcomes Satan in the form of a serpent in a vibrant relief figure at St. Michael Church in Paterson, New Jersey (above). The statue of St. Paul the Apostle (left) adorns the dramatic entranceway to St. Paul's Cathedral in Pittsburgh, Pennsylvania. Also known as the "Missionary to the Gentiles," he holds a sword—symbolic of his martyrdom—and the scroll of his Epistles. On the opposite page, gargoyles—fantastic creatures commonly seen on medieval European cathedrals, usually symbolizing worldly or evil forces that are subdued by angels above—ornament the Calvary United Methodist Church in Pittsburgh, Pennsylvania.

Gable and Spire Ornaments

On the opposite page, wooden crosses and finials crown the Scandinavian Björklunden Chapel in Door County, Wisconsin. Above, left: a rooster weathervane perches above the classical cupola with balustrade of the West Parish Church, in West Barnstable, Massachusetts; above, right, a rayed and gilded globe adorns the steeple of the Trinity Church in Washington Depot, Connecticut. At right, a rugged Celtic cross centers on the Greek letters *Alpha* and *Omega* (the Beginning and the End), symbolic of Christ, in Morristown, New Jersey.

Axis Mundi

Rhythmic upright forms speak to the role of sacred places as symbolic links between earth and heaven. Above is a quadruple reflection of the handsome Gothic spire of St. Paul's Cathedral in Pittsburgh, Pennsylvania. On the opposite page, the Greek Revival façade of the First Congregational Church of Ellsworth, Maine, features Ionic columns. At right is an eclectic shingled steeple on the Church of the Assumption in Westport, Connecticut.

Belfries: Hail and Farewell

Time-honored belfries that have called congregations to
worship, rejoice and grieve together: above is a detail of
the San Juan Bautista Mission (1797), California, with
red-tiled roof and triple belfry; at right is a free-standing
bell-tower in the cemetery of a Federal-style church in
Alexandria, Virginia. On the opposite page is a peaceful
New England cemetery beside its nineteenth-century
Congregational Church.

Glossary of Architectural Terms

acanthus leaf A stylized Mediterranean leaf form used as decoration, especially for Corinthian **capitals**.

apse A semicircular or vaulted projection from a church building, usually containing the sanctuary, or chancel, where the altar is located.

arcade A series of arches on columns or **piers** supporting a wall.

ashlar A square-cut stone masonry, usually laid in even courses.

balustrade A low rail supported by short posts.

basilica A rectangular building designed along a longitudinal axis, leading from a **narthex** through a central **nave** to an **apse** containing the sanctuary.

bay The vertical sections projecting from a façade, usually featuring three or more windows.

bellcast roof A roof that flares out at the eaves, typical of French architecture.

board and batten The wooden sheathing of wide vertical boards alternating with narrow strips of wood, called battens, that cover the joints.

bracket A small projecting piece of stone or wood that supports a horizontal member, e.g., the eaves.

buttress An exterior masonry support built into or against a wall to strengthen it.

capital The crowning member of a column, **pier**, or shaft in the classical **orders**.

clapboard A narrow board used to cover frame buildings.

colonnade A row of regularly spaced columns, usually supporting an **entablature** and part of a roof.

cornice A projecting molding that crowns the top of a building.

crenelation The notched or indented tops of walls and towers, typical of the Tudor Revival and similar medieval styles.

crocket A decorative roof ornament, usually in leaf shape, commonly found in Gothic Revival architecture.

cupola A small dome or other rooftop structure that sometimes serves as a belfry or for ventilation.

entablature The horizontal beams, sometimes decorated, resting on columns or **pilasters**.

finial A vertical ornament at the top of a gable or roofline.

frieze A wide band of ornamental forms, usually carved in relief.

gambrel roof A ridged roof with two slopes on each side.

hipped roof A roof with four pitched sides.

iconostasis A partition or screen separating the sanctuary from the main part of an Eastern Orthodox church, hung with icons, or sacred images.

keystone The central stone at the apex of an arch or vault.

lancet A narrow pointed Gothic window.

lintel The horizontal beam spanning the top of a door or window opening.

lunette A semicircular window.

narthex The porch or entrance hall preceding the main hall in a place of worship.

nave The open central space in a place of worship, often flanked by aisles and/or galleries.

order An arrangement of columns and **entablature** in classical Greek architecture, categorized as Doric, Ionic and Corinthian.

pediment The triangular gable end of a classical-style building; also seen over windows and doorways.

pier A heavy stone or brick support, usually square or rectangular in form.

pilaster A rectangular or rounded column projecting slightly from a wall.

portico A covered porch or walkway supported by columns.

quoin A protruding stone or brick patterned to accentuate exterior corners and façade openings.

rib A slender arched support in Romanesque and Gothic vaults.

rose window A circular window with radiating **tracery** or glazing bars, often filled with stained glass.

spire The slender, sharply pointed summit of a tower or roof.

stringcourse A protruding horizontal band along the façade of a building, used to define the story levels; also called belt course.

tracery The branching ornamental stone- or woodwork commonly used in Gothic-style windows to support the glass.

transept The section of a cruciform church that crosses at right angles to the greatest length between the **nave** and the sanctuary, or chancel.

trefoil A three-lobed cloverleaf pattern.

Tudor arch A shallow pointed arch seen in late-medieval English architecture.

vault The covering over an arched area; various shapes include the semicircular or barrel vault of Romanesque architecture, and the Gothic fan vault, in a concave, conical shape.

Index

Bibliography

Chiat, Marilyn J. *America's Religious Architecture: Sacred Places for Every Community.* New York: John Wiley & Sons, 1997.

Diamondstein, Barbara Lee. *The Landmarks of New York.* New York: Harry N. Abrams, 1988.

Dixon, Roger, and Stefan Muthesius. *Victorian Architecture.* World of Art series. London: Thames and Hudson, 1978.

Kennedy, Roger G. *American Churches.* New York: Stewart, Tabori & Chang, 1982.

Lawless, Chuck. *The Old West Sourcebook.* New York: Crown Publishers, 1994.

Leonard, Roger M. *The Red Church.* Tivoli, New York: St. Paul's Episcopal Church, 1990.

Maitland, Leslie, et al. *A Guide to Canadian Architectural Styles.* Peterborough, Ontario: Broadview Press, 1992.

Packard, Robert, and Balthazar Korab. *Encyclopedia of American Architecture,* 2nd ed. New York: McGraw-Hill, 1995.

Sinnott, Edmund W. *Meetinghouse & Church in Early New England.* New York: McGraw-Hill, 1963.

Upton, Dell, ed. *America's Architectural Roots: Ethnic Groups That Built America,* Building Watchers series. Washington, D.C.: National Trust for Historic Preservation, 1986.

Waterhouse, P. Leslie. *The Story of Architecture,* 3rd ed., British Art and Building Series. London: B.T. Batsford Ltd., 1950.

White, Norval. *New York: A Physical History.* New York: Atheneum/Macmillan, 1987.

Acknowledgements

The publisher would like to thank the following individuals for their assistance in the preparation of this book: Sara Hunt and Nicola J. Gillies, editors; Charles J. Ziga, art director and photographer; Wendy Ciaccia Eurell, graphic designer; Lisa Langone Desautels, indexer; Jay Olstad for supplementary research and photography; and Annie Lise Roberts for her architecture expertise. Grateful acknowledgement is also made to the communities of the featured churches, travel and tourism agencies, historical societies across the continent and the photographers and agencies listed below for permission to reproduce the photographs on the following pages: © Kindra Clineff 1999: 2, 4–5, 11, 12, 15t, 25, 26, 32, 44–45, 81, 141; © Robert Drapala: 50, 55; © Rudi Holnsteiner: 39, 43, 52b, 56, 59t, 60, 61, 68–69 (both), 70–71 (all), 72t, 74, 75t, 85t, 87b, 99, 105, 111, 114b, 126, 140t; © Balthazar Korab: 9, 42 (both), 57, 73, 84, 87t, 92, 97b, 109b, 110, 127, 140b; © Jay Olstad: 18b, 57, 77, 94b, 98t, 130, 132t; © Michael A. Smith: 40, 125 (both); © John Sylvester 21, 38, 48, 49, 63, 65, 88–89, 90, 91, 115, 117t, 120t, 121, 133; © Charles J. Ziga: 1, 6, 7, 10, 14, 15b, 16, 17, 18–19t, 19b, 20 (both), 22, 23, 24, 28–29 (all), 30, 31, 35, 36 (both), 37, 41, 46–47t, 51 (both), 52t, 54b, 58, 59b, 62, 64b, 66, 67, 75b, 76, 79, 80, 82, 83 (both), 85b, 86, 93 (both), 94t, 95, 96, 97t, 100, 101, 102, 103, 104, 106–107 (both), 108, 112, 113 (both), 114t, 116, 117b, 118, 119b, 120b, 122, 123, 124 (both), 128–129 (all), 131 (both), 132b, 134 (both), 135, 137 (all), 138–139 (all); FPG International, LLC: 46b (© Jeri Gleiter 1995), 109t (© Peter Gridley 1997), 119t (© Dennie Cody 1996); Santa Fe CVB: 8 (© Chris Corrie); Vermont Department of Tourism and Marketing: 27, 33, 34, 78, 98b; Wisconsin Department of Tourism: 136.